Australian Animals
Bandicoots

by Lyn A. Sirota

Consulting Editor: Gail Saunders-Smith, PhD

Content Consultant: Amanda Watson
Senior Biodiversity Officer, Department of Sustainability and Environment
Victoria, Australia

CAPSTONE PRESS
a capstone imprint

Pebble Plus is published by Capstone Press,
151 Good Counsel Drive, P.O. Box 669, Mankato, Minnesota 56002.
www.capstonepub.com

 Books published by Capstone Press are manufactured with paper containing at least 10 percent post-consumer waste.

Library of Congress Cataloging-in-Publication Data
Sirota, Lyn A., 1963-
    Bandicoots / by Lyn A. Sirota.
    p. cm. — (Pebble plus. Australian animals)
    Includes bibliographical references and index.
    Summary: "Simple text and photographs present bandicoots, their physical features, where they live, and what they do" — Provided by publisher.
    ISBN 978-1-4296-4503-4 (library binding)
    1. Bandicota — Juvenile literature. I. Title. II. Series.
QL737.R666S567 2010
599.2'6 — dc22   2009040491

Editorial Credits
Gillia Olson, editor; Bobbie Nuytten, designer; Wanda Winch, media researcher; Eric Manske, production specialist

Photo Credits
Alamy/Arco Images GmbH/K. Mosebach, 13
Ardea/Hans and Judy Beste, 9
Corbis/Martin Harvey, 7; Steve Kaufman, 5
Lochman Transparencies/©Jiri Lochman, PD-135, 21; RF-095, cover, 19; ZF-007, 1
Peter Arnold/Biosphoto/J.-L. Klein & M.-L. Hubert, 15
Photo Researchers, Inc/ANT Photo Library, 11, 17

Note to Parents and Teachers

The Australian Animals set supports national science standards related to life science. This book describes and illustrates bandicoots. The images support early readers in understanding the text. The repetition of words and phrases helps early readers learn new words. This book also introduces early readers to subject-specific vocabulary words, which are defined in the Glossary section. Early readers may need assistance to read some words and to use the Table of Contents, Glossary, Read More, Internet Sites, and Index sections of the book.

Printed in the United States of America in North Mankato, Minnesota.
022011   006080R

Table of Contents

Living in Australia

Bandicoots are bunny-sized marsupials hopping through Australia's backyards. They weigh up to 4.5 pounds (2 kilograms).

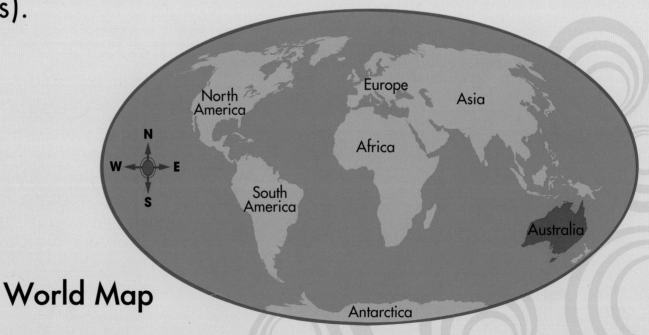

World Map

Bandicoots live in Australia's woodlands, grasslands, and deserts.
By day, they rest in nests.
At night, they hunt.

Australia Map

where bandicoots live

Up Close!

Long pointy noses help

bandicoots sniff out prey.

Their long tongues

snatch grubs to eat.

Sharp teeth crunch beetles.

Bandicoots have short front legs and long back legs. Long claws help bandicoots dig for food.

Food and Water

Bandicoots eat grubs, worms,

plants, and berries.

Bandicoots get most

of their water from their food.

13

Growing Up

Female bandicoots give birth to up to four young at one time. The young are called joeys. Joeys stay safe in their mother's pouch for about eight weeks.

Joeys spend two weeks with

their mother out of the pouch.

Then joeys live on their own.

Bandicoots can have

up to four litters a year.

Predators

Bandicoots hide from predators.
But bandicoots' main predators
are not native to Australia.
Foxes, dogs, and cats find
and easily prey on bandicoots.

As people use land, bandicoots
have fewer places to live.
Laws protect all bandicoots
so they'll always be able
to hop around Australia.

Glossary

grub — a young form of an insect that looks like a short, white worm

joey — a young bandicoot

litter — a group of young born to one mother at the same time

marsupial — a mammal that carries its young in a pouch

native — originally from a certain place; foxes, cats, and dogs are not originally from Australia; settlers brought them.

pouch — a pocket of skin; bandicoot joeys live in their mother's pouch.

predator — an animal that hunts other animals for food

prey — to hunt another animal for food

Read More

Kalman, Bobbie, and Hadley Dyer. *Australian Outback Food Chains*. Food Chains. New York: Crabtree, 2007.

Kras, Sara Louise. *Kangaroos*. Australian Animals. Mankato, Minn.: Capstone Press, 2009.

Votaw, Carol J. *Waking Up Down Under*. Minnetonka, Minn.: NorthWord Books for Young Readers, 2007.

Internet Sites

FactHound offers a safe, fun way to find Internet sites related to this book. All of the sites on FactHound have been researched by our staff.

Here's all you do:

Visit *www.facthound.com*

FactHound will fetch the best sites for you!

Index

Word Count: 185
Grade: 1
Early-Intervention Level: 20